Kieran Clarke is a writer with a message! His poetry and writings are fresh, dynamic and multi-dimensional. Kieran has struggled with considerable mental health problems for much of his life and in his darkest moments received the light of inspiration to well up from within himself words that evoke a deep transformational possibility of what can be positively achieved and realized through tapping into our innate wisdom. He wishes to shed light on the power that words can have to catapult a suffering soul into viewing life with a reversed perception.

My twinflame Daniella, my son, Kaiden, and to all those who are seeking liberation from mental slavery and distress!

Kieran Clarke

QUANTUM AWAKENING

WORDS OF TRANSFORMATION

AUSTIN MACAULEY PUBLISHERS™

LONDON · CAMBRIDGE · NEW YORK · SHARJAH

A CIP catalogue record for this title is available from the British Library.

ISBN 9781398403956 (Paperback)
ISBN 9781398403963 (ePub e-book)

www.austinmacauley.com

First Published 2021
Austin Macauley Publishers Ltd®
1 Canada Square
Canary Wharf
London
E14 5AA

Author's Note

This book is a collection of my personal writings or poetry that delve deep into the metaphysical and spiritual realms of human existence. I have used metaphors and complex play-on-words that will allow an open interpretation to each individual. The purpose of my writings is to allow people to connect deeply with their own spirit and prompt inner enlightenment within their own lives. I believe these writings come from a higher sphere and were in many ways channelled through me for the betterment of all readers.

Intro

Welcome, reader. If you have found your way to this book then you are called to hear the messages of your soul; the mystic words of your unfathomable spirit.

These words are mystical and metaphysical poetry and were penned mostly during my admissions in hospital and during times of expansiveness; I wrote this because deep channellings and communications were occurring within me and I was prompted to write; it is a book of awakening, transformation and the keys to access alternate dimensions within your life, thus helping you remember that you are a multi-dimensional being. May my insights into the depth of the infinite universe within us bless you and keep you liberated.

Glowing

The re-emergence of the latter-day quantum awakenings subliminally enrich and impart visual messages via tuned-in transmissions of grandeur.

Open the spacious cavern into which space embraces a sensation of measurement that will not transform without her! Trust within loss, no idleness can prevent the opening in which no man can shut.

The electrical consciousness will sustain me.

The solution which pervades the time-trap is ever-glowing. Empty fullness spits ions down through auditory compassion.

Summon the courage of a lion, as a garden springs into life. Spirit in the sky, spirit in the heart. Encrusted secrets demanding their song to be heard.

It's the final gap. A woven tapestry liberating mental torture into a river of flowing life.

Ever present confusion. Dying to a sword of thorns as fertilized love takes over!

Wireless

Aggressive lessons, attacked and pillaged, ripped in all directions. Summoning a defiant stance; chronic self-defence, enemies exasperated by the sword within my mind.

The wind is our mother, opening a transformer of self-generated vibration. Obscure passengers inflating her life-force through a maze of opportunity. Observed silence, breaking as a dam into wild, improvised explosions. The purple hand of a star friend.

Deeply impressed notion, one eye injection, peace into an unbridled mess. Native wisdom sings and beats deep in the mountain halls. Why reverse your smile? It keeps planets in order!

Never alone in the wilderness, perfected stance, stable and solid light movements, waving through a reflected rainbow at a heart etched in stone. Vibrate furiously, abrupt supernovas call for home!

Parted images, victorious signs waging war in the heavens. Sublime submission surrendering emptiness into fullness! Intensive nerve connections, the words of ancestors.

Tongue in cheek majesty, mass elixir!

Dream Space

A melodic bubble infused with divine breath. Empowered substance never disintegrating into brokenness. Cathartic heart-wrecks sink infinitely only to rise once more. Rhythmic subtleties blossom inspiration into never-ending starlight!

She will carry on, breakthroughs will follow her every step, her emptiness can only become whole as a smile returns to her soul. Never-despairing, she will find a way, guided by angels, never going astray. I will hold her hand and with two feet stand. I will watch her transform and never deform as her heart explodes with love and warmth.

Feminine

She fills my void, deep flourishing. Flickers of hope speak within her soul. Her hand, electric, her heart summons my love as a warrior to battle. Her rhythm is my blues. I caress her pain as she enlightens my fears. Intensity like no other, her radiance provokes a rainfall of tears in my humble heart. I hear her natural yet supernatural music playing symphonies, infusing confusion with clarity. Faith growing from a seed, she moves inner mountains with just her glance. Hold on to me dear, my surprise is to set my love free. Melodic changes shift in amazing arrays behind her smile. My spirit is saved as I rest my head upon your delicate love!

Darkness

The dark lizard becoming a wizard for effortless manifestation. Star truths unravelled gentle miracles within the heart chamber. His darkest disciple protects me with a fury. Blurred lines intercepting solid appearances. Full spectrum opulence of the crystal, ever growing ferocity against lower vibrations. Prayer of the child, opening a cloned innocence for super soul radiance.

He speaks with authority; I am your sword amidst the undying mists. Never interrupted. Insane sanity, washing his mind as he glows intensely. I receive from his lord downloads of spirit and music; this is all that remains. Inspired in stone, incorruptible wonder. Floating lanterns below the mirror pool. Why envisage such grandeur? His sword listens, his blood inscribes power!

Forms

32 mystical forms, giving word for his awakened survival. Learning to speak again, creating substance, vibration of the doubles amidst his geometry. Singing life speaks truth. The rumble of formlessness. An empty signal heeding a perception shift! Integral potions brewing a detached chase, prepared for supernova.

Concealing nothing, kneeling on his battle-field with everything that his sword can sing. Infinite death giving rise to joyful hymns. Detached fuel engraving emergence!

Sacred

Mysterious friend, spectral intelligence, tuned into unseen realms.

The empty realm, stars of light! Conveying energetic palm magic. Elemental-verse crying for space and space they shall obtain. Infinite painted talents, speak in smoke with multiple observances. Deeply enriched vigour.

Dwelling in his empty realm, completely unafraid, deeply moved into succession. Freedom from thought!

Established extinction. Sacred incantation.

Thanksgiving

Hunger residing!

Dreams of awakening, pushing negative illusion away. Seeking breath and infinite expression. Denying life's intrusions; experience of both sides indefinitely.

Door wide open, rushing waters of the misty valley. Transmissions of higher frequency into love substance. Increasing explosive ocean love. Infinite light body. Crystal speaks, listen!

Deep thanksgiving, joyful transmissions, honour among frequencies! Peace!

Desert Rose, implied marriage! Feeling overwhelmed by love, essential and fundamental requirements, offspring conceived in love, heavenly support, full assistance! Dropping control, harmonizing wills. Empty stillness in motion. Higher love frequencies.

Influences

Encased switch, powerful non-response, compassionate sword! Indestructible congruence merging at zero, travelling unhindered with vast potential.

High freedoms, open receptions, mechanical fluidity enlightening offerings of his super-soul. Effortless attainment of wind messages, solidified by word, intended by love.

Abundant confidence within love its very self. Controlled influences, inspired influence. Traversing waves dispel material concerns.

Follow his map! Peace!

Great compassion arising in joy. May the great fathers within the halls await our return to the undying lands. All balanced words in love represents powerful reflections on an immense scale.

Heroes

Return to inner freedom, great freedom, inspired hand connection, embracing death with pure life. Extinction of all fear. Ever-present word, soft echoes in the silence.

He arises now with a balanced fury. He has awoken, now he shall love himself unto death!

Intercepting heroic Euphoria as a hero's welcome! Star formation, ancient shape. Energy healed, ions, ancient and silent. Secret distance, dashed communication. Ever-ready to speak. Explosive truths.

Colours

Enquiring breath. Expanded colour, once caged, broken free. Tapped currencies now in true fullness.

Seven generations, blessed angel, arms open in receptive love amidst unspeakable pain. Outpouring of the mother spirit, spectrum of smiles enduring blessings to all, a passing breeze of compassion, igniting hope and injecting light in those despairing. A rainbow angel, makes a home in broken hearts.

Silent Warrior

Silent warrior, ever awake and subtle in his movements. Alone always, yet infinitely connected. Open powers, a love with no name, heart exploding in unseen territory! Hold his hand, unshakable joy within darkness.

Every time he spreads his wings, my heart aches with a broken love. Unto death he sheds tears, violet and all consuming.

Reading his soul amidst the ambush; bright and open even as his crown becomes thorns, he expands forgiveness.

Wrapped in a blanket of ocean comfort. Steps quiet and silent even as he awoke. Praying to his father above, such roses are his very own.

The sword of thorns cuts portals, piercing healing truth. Overflowing cup of delight. Heavens erase messages and frame them in blue ink. As winter approaches, quantum stars radiate autumn colours. How can my hand create such harmony as a message electrified?

Contained lamps, offering hidden music to all! Wondrous approach of mystical tones. Never ashamed of the constant glow.

His blessings turn within, enriching powerful storms of creation. Openly floating, peace abounds.

Reduced

Protection as compassion. Never will one fall into darkness. Enrichment as an eye opener. Love expands, enveloping all darkness. Never fear this unfolding. Carried through the stars. Plasma mother cradling a lost son. Climbing ever-more into the depths of heaven. Never ceasing to be joyfully present.

Reduced to truth through her light, entering her orbit with my legions of warriors, sealing her atmosphere, spearing through her defiled layers, allowing our lights to merge.

Ancestor

Gifted to her realm, vases of constellations pulsing coils reward the empty light! Devoid of blue sparkle, an indent of anxious time!

Convoluted conclave of enticed persuasion. Ever-green tears of multiplication. Fierce forward momentum. We implore a sweet efficiency through our vessel. Ancestral pre-occupation diverse as love's nucleus. Enter my rhythmic confusion to find peace. Use the engine of my word, let it carry you through the Bardo of illusory existence.

Mother colours slip and bi-locate within cosmic hills. Soul fragments crying into completion. Inverted visions of grandeur. Why run, my child? The empty gifts are your birth right. A word and a star rest gently in your officious will!

Shadows

The fading shadows disperse in the wake of your indestructible light. Immerse your angels with gentle messages. Quantum entanglement ensures our survival. Creaking constitutions slay oncoming threat. All darkness will enter quarantine. You shall see the rising sun and your eyes shall beam with a rejoiced vigour. Changeable expressions pluck ethereal strings. White noise becomes your comfort when you abide in non-substantiality.

Receive the space. Green Tara in essence everywhere. Perceptions of victory glide inward and end as a melted wave.

The undercurrent raging within the under-belly. Her subtle movements eliminate crossed intentions. Invade my heart, request residence as my independence becomes co-dependant.

Spectral

Crystalline interpretations of immersive diverse surrender. Implore new offerings, measuring his love beyond the veil. Welcome, wayfarer, into my peripheral pensive amusement. Encrypt foreign wordsmiths, apply conscious unlocking of our grateful awareness. Embracing imperative pain for simple peace. Clear sight emanating shooting puzzles, colourful spectral borders, passing all through with heartfelt acceptance. Hold them, gently guide. Smiling effortlessly, a bombardment of unexpected compassion! Open plains, enclosed vacuum singing behind the cheek of a confused star! Don't aim infinitely at the oppressed. Spontaneous eruption performing for an empty crowd. Rotary words ground passively hand in hand!

Illusions

Musical classes of red. Reaching far into a shallow venture. Refracted illusions remove the strife. Solid love beneath my feet. Inter-locked epiphanies explode as a rose emerges under trickled light.

Hello stranger, sing for her, write for her, hold her. Ever-impressed, transient lessons teaching us a new way. Don't leave the heart's embrace, it rains endlessly. You have healed my need; a white blossoming, never detached, forever awake.

Gravity

Forever harmonious. Envisioned heaven, convoluted waves of heightened awareness. The divine cross appears in glory upon the throne as the elders bask in the joy of loves' mighty image. Standing firm amidst heavens distinct supplication. Heaven's trusted heart beckons furiously with her son's love, impress indefinitely with a gravitation above, through and beyond the inner stars. The visitors increase my substitute forever in one changeable glory. Inexpressible and voracious tactician and physician! Compressed radiance clears my way into the light above.

Untethered

An untethered soul, walking in love's valley. Her distinct majesty humbles his pure spirit. Entrance to the halls of wonder, seeking movement in the still images. Welcoming with open arms, a gift is received with conscious gratitude.

Trapped in the present moment, free and still, naturally arising love and compassion.

The great law, impermanence, empty yet full! Salvation through the great vessel!

Liberation of Suffering

Wide open expanse, freeing my mind. Existing fiercely as a created light, never mind my lower self, it has no say in my power. Trust in me and open my eyes, follow this path and never look back. My instrument is suffering, can you not see my friend? My dear friend. They cannot harm you again, my dear friend, my dear friend!

Existing on a turntable, infinitely imbalanced and casually toying with freedom. Solid life playing with your vibration as presence arises like a roaring lion. Crossing the river with open eyes and external faith. Images burn with song!

Craving Surrender

Without supplication, I am entering deeper into the dream spirit. Stronger I am through a depth of compassion and humility, connecting the strings of awareness. Concurrent boundlessness enriches the teacher's student. A life apart from lies becomes tender. The seed sprouts forth tenderness. Given the life of the word, miracles breath in perfect order. As the strings tighten, no longer can fear rule our spheres of existence.

Fertility

Musical imbalance lights my laughter. Encourage my reasons for deciphering purpose. Expanse moves within circles. Allowing her fertility to soften edges. A sage moves unerringly upon an unseen road. Unnerved and solid, a truth among heroes, gallant and piercing!

She teases my soul with a smile. Dances with my light in the shadows like a lone candle flickering in the dark. She frees me like a bird yet captures me when I fly too high. A force of creativity when the show ends, a spark of truth when confusion appears. An upheaval of silent, charged emotion meshes as the night's emptiness hugs the stars. Shudders awake my sleeping heart as she draws near. Her hand is a crutch, a canal in which my weakness can flow when in need. Time learns to obey when she weaves her choppy web, my expanse is honoured! She counsels my incentives, cradles my wanderings and inspires a burning for her return to stability. Extinguish my secrets, dissipate my frailties, allow me to display my multiple lights so as to illumine your perceptions of my transparency. Condensing my factual astral juices, so you can taste with rippled texture the inspiration of gravitational reflections.

Constructs

Positive expanse, uplifting highs. Ethereal tentacles blessing my mind. Spacious continuum lights up our stillness. Thankful projections cleanse hurts. Ascended forgiveness enriches a cloudy view.

Invalidated constructs Eclipse our mind! Indifferent sameness elopes symmetrically. Giving rise to infinite harmonizing. Rise up, blind child, open your sight and dance once again, smile.

Geometric Connections float gloriously upon my head. The rainbow body elucidates my powerful stillness as we invest heavily in the now. Riches of totality!

My hollow saviour, embracing all within the emptiness, no form, no sensation, wrapped in impermanence, expressible using tools of the void for perfect clarity.

Butterfly

Empty space, a friend to my ideas, a limitless cause to call freedom, a cage unknown, a vast sky, my sacred monastery. Dispersed connections, quiet knowledge, imparted yet forgotten. Wind and rain emanating from breath. Signals raised via the butterfly. In their multitudes they arrive, impressed with cloaks of the directed word. Never awake, always still as they run. Bridges built as a hidden mind valley. The method of impartation as a congested spirit never abounding. Distorted remnants creep lovingly back to their masters. Lily of the valley embracing lost sheep.

Trust

Conveyed collaborations amplify the waves of inspiration. Invested percussion gives rise to smooth textures. Upheld by five dimensional portraits, the sentient within can charge ferociously with full intent.

Immense sensations of release. Conveyed feelings of love. Untouchable inspirations manifesting effortlessly. Seamless fortitude, condensed equilibrium. Contorted space stretching unendingly without plan. Divinity touched by full trust.

Continuum

The fiery prophets uphold my insanity. Freeing lives of torment for good. Effortless abundance, a process of internal cleaning. Uphold my needs and always I will erase your problem memories. Reflective work, transmuting all issues. Come to me, you who are burdened and peace you shall learn.

Kindly pursuing endurance, endeavouring too persevere. Open valleys, free-flowing streams of validated star dust. Ever-glowing mists of time fill the empty space. Invoke my heart and heed its message!

Continuum of my galaxy, spectral overshadows whisper names of life.

Follow my resting ways, laughing reverently with vibration.

King

As they swept by, we acknowledged the face of the king. Reverently taking back dominion of the freedom of word. Consistently upholding through the void. Sparking into reality the visions of colour. Freedom in all respects. Infected with love. Never abounding a simplicity of prophecy, engaged traveller. He is colour, healing music and born without fear.

Find your balance between life and death!

Re-emergence

A creative imagination, temporarily conductive, the seeds of awakening. Fearless emotive imaginings awoke and blossomed intuitively as the wave became the ocean. Thanksgiving breeds truth in my entangled heart. Advise my informative mind garden. Trust within life, within death. Carry this seed and grow it with sound, illumine the dark skies as salt within lightening.

Infinite skyrockets, enamel through the pores, a genius, silent, without form. Increased convulsions at peace. Shamanic re-emergence as the keys to prosper. Creative intuition as the father holds my hand. A prophet awakening enlists my freedom. A silent witch, momentarily irradiating fuzz!

Living Waters

Engines of molecular hidings. Uploaded informative opening of doors. The spirit watcher settles my soul. The ceiling will be touched and the portals of loving communication instructs higher levels of living waters. The sky accepts our reflection in my own time. Bent messages!

Buttered footsteps glide through my invisible desires. An offering to my mountains, my rivers and construed liberations. Speak through me as I contemplate and look into you. Three constraints unrestrained. Revealing my natures, sparks of electricity in my inter-dimensional running's.

Blooming

Intricate spaces, illuminated prophesy filled with a connection beyond the multiverse. Detected transmissions of ventilated light! Tunnels ferry the neurons of the silver light. Incorporating the vase of growth, spontaneous eruption, a spectacular bloom.

Delicate love, gentle awareness, magical movements, a life-giving gift! A hero rests amidst big battles.

Invasive growth, past jewels transforming into explosive abundance! Heart language evokes the need to communicate a raging stream of nourishing waters. Howling for change, howling for peaceful justice.

I Am Enough

When battles ensue, I am enough! When devils twist, I am enough. When higher self is compromised, I am enough! When life becomes real, I am Enough.

Mystery

Self-pertained mysteries of consciousness. Open Plasticity of the illusory constructs held within life's humbled appearance. Hold their hands with magnified joy. Star friends entitle our grace. Waiting patiently as static becomes crystal with direct communication. Thank you!

They came to me by the riverside. Mystic tongues spoke over and entered my spirit as colours to heal. An exclusive interval awoke my inner eye. I revelled in the majesty never subsiding or overriding the call.

As the black womb creates space for the allowance of my creation, infinite cheer springs forth above my praying shell.

Glimpses

Windows give a glimpse through the etheric realm of centred knowingness. Reflecting home, the rainbow of geometric temples. We arise gladly, radiant as rays of purity. Dispelling all fear time and time again until all that remains is timeless, unborn reflective bliss!

Oily spectrums evading all capture. Unveil their heart, touch compassion, new situation, new blessings. My pen unleashes a spectral reality of imaginative peace, never let go, never jump off!

Great Vessel

As portals of my forefathers embark heroically towards our ancestral home, I can only imagine you peacefully flowing onwards. Honestly flowing, honestly silent, honestly safe.

Overflowing emotive strength, listen intently, we can hear your heart song, never fear! Intelligent mood swings variate the lesson. Ferociously amazed. Revitalised comments within his tender dream. Plausible and small, never falling, please perceive, perceive, perceive!

Grass grows, notes enrich, a song kills falseness, the great vessel speaks.

Companions

Smallest infinite sky radiating peaceful assurances. Linear lectures posing as your life. Lifting darkness, evaporating shadows, a joy most surely ferocious with no notion of fear. Incredible fiery torches emitting wholesome freedom for many to bathe in.

Growth immeasurable for gifted tacticians! Healing fluid and harmonious actions. Ever-watchful friend, devoid of judgement. Glass symphony of gritty tones.

Unseen companions, stationed at all posts. Gabriel with a sword of ethereal substances. Flooding joy as broken is repaired. Vibrating stillness becomes a stray's guiding beacon!

Focused eyes, piercing and locked, never wavering, lifted towards your inner heaven!

Supplication, unfolding will! Granted abundantly to open hands. Gracious acceptance!

Crossed cleansing evaporates christened laziness.

Electrical Realities

Inter-dimensional realities within the electrical human. Evoking openings of primordial light sent inwards, touching the heaven within and magnetising the neuroplastic heart sun. Journeying ferociously with intermittent pulses conveying light messages altering the empty, impermanent states of being. Levitating notions running haywire, being of humble knowledge open the floodgates within the hidden realms of a changed mind. Transcendent vibrations rattling the bars of freedom collide as entangled particles. Bravely standing firm whilst sweetly surrendering the non-return of being. Mystical starlight swooping an image of continuity! Manipulated matter conferring an obstinate determination of heightened persuasion. Dying cells become divine action resting within the buzzing current of human connectivity.

Message

It's a pure light. Running freely across vast plains and endless ocean images. Conclave decisions produce results worth breathing for. The actor expresses his inner-most being. All spectators resist spontaneous joy for the fear of ridicule. You are the light!

The Empty Thought

Misty visions, illusions in the dark. I am the open door which no man can shut. Cleansed and re-wired. Divining the subtle art of cosmic transcendence! Allowing Frugality!

Troubled ease communicating effortlessly with the loving spirit.

The End!